BABY AVIVA
ORANGUTAN DIVA

by Hans Kullberg
Illustrated by Carl Mefferd

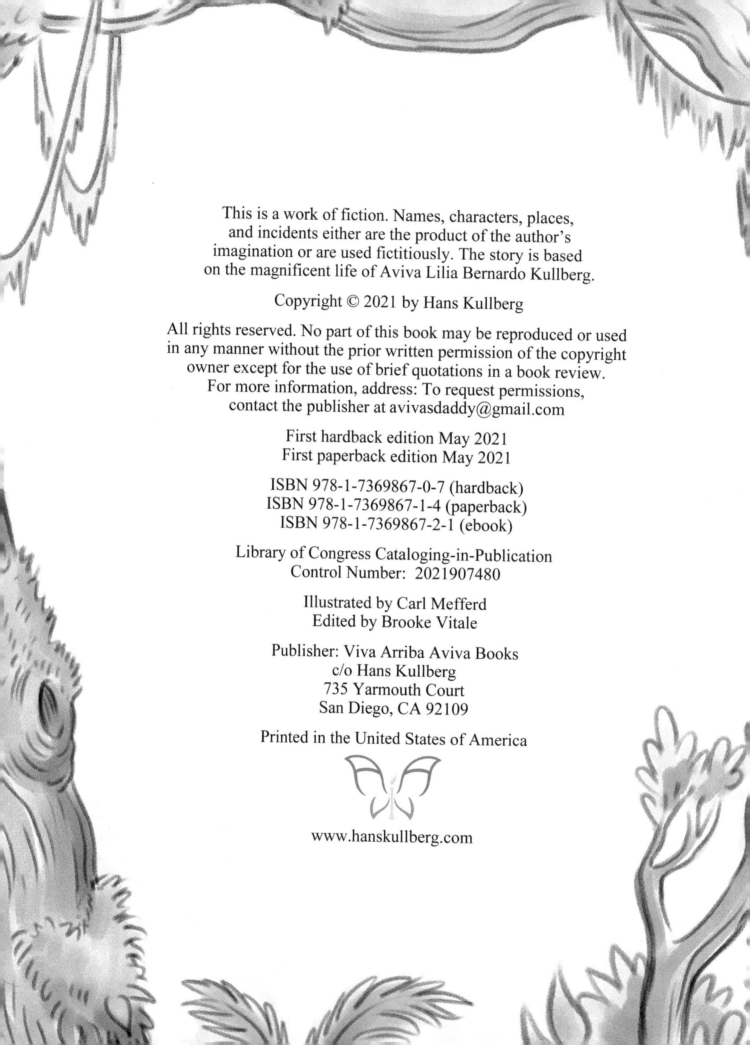

First hardback edition May 2021
First paperback edition May 2021

ISBN 978-1-7369867-0-7 (hardback)
ISBN 978-1-7369867-1-4 (paperback)
ISBN 978-1-7369867-2-1 (ebook)

Library of Congress Cataloging-in-Publication
Control Number: 2021907480

Illustrated by Carl Mefferd
Edited by Brooke Vitale

Publisher: Viva Arriba Aviva Books
c/o Hans Kullberg
735 Yarmouth Court
San Diego, CA 92109

Printed in the United States of America

www.hanskullberg.com

For my dearest daughter,
Aviva Lilia, who continues to inspire
me from up above.

Smile down upon us always,
Sunshine Aviva.

Yeeee Haaaaaawwwwww!!!

Out of the darkness
and into the light
a rocket, comet
or maybe a star so bright?

Swinging from treetops
was Baby Aviva.

Just two feet tall,
the Orangutan Diva.

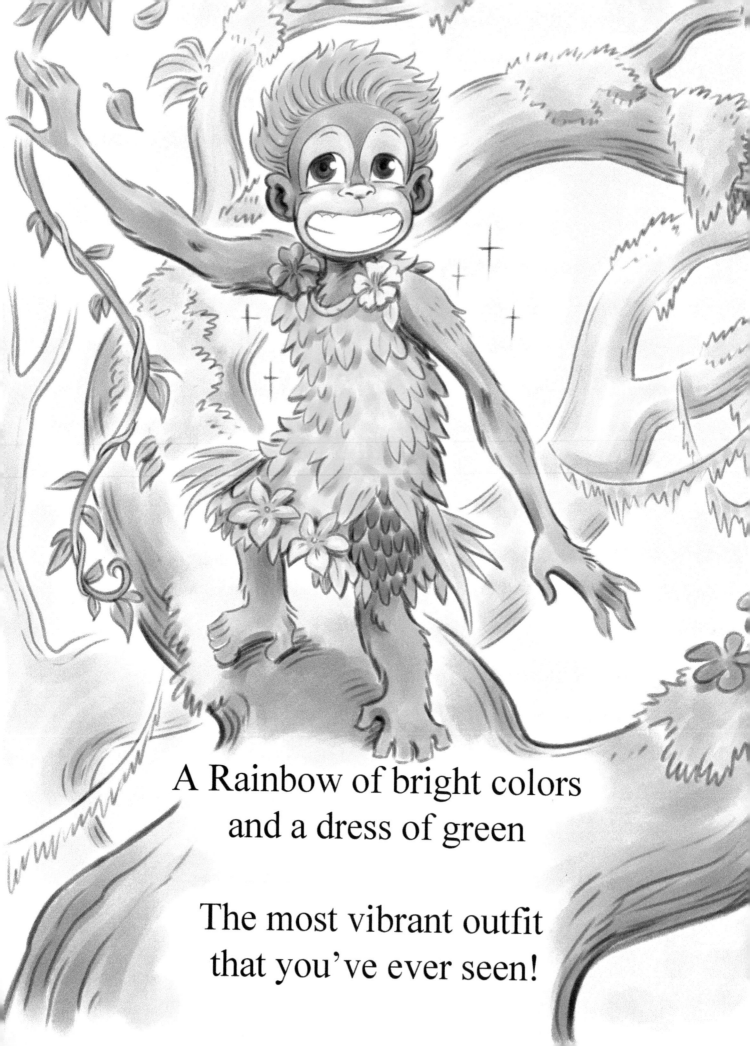

A Rainbow of bright colors
and a dress of green

The most vibrant outfit
that you've ever seen!

Zipping on down
from the tops of the trees,

"Good morning!" she sang
to the birds and the bees.

Her voice rang out clearly,
a sweet little tune,

Her melody carried
right up to the moon!

Tummy a-rumbling,
she did a shimmy down a tree.

She searched for bananas,
but…where could they be?

Hard as she looked,
there were none to be found.

"Holy Moly Guacamole!" she cried;
her jaw dropping to the ground

"We're out of bananas?
No, that can't be right.

Maybe they're just hiding
out of our sight?"

"It's true, I'm afraid," Mama said with a frown
"We must cross the river,
though I fear we might drown!"

She was right – No Ape, Monkey
or Goat had crossed in quite some time
For the tigers were roaming
and crocs were waiting in line

But the timing was urgent,
her family was out of food

"I'll go," said Aviva,
"Is anyone else in such a brave mood?"

"I'll come!" said Sofia. "I'm brave and I'm strong. I'll help you to cross with my trunk, ten-feet long"

"Great! Nothing's too scary for my friend Sofia and I We'll pluck those bananas right out of the sky!"

So off the two went,
across the raging river
A place that nobody dared go,
and barely even said with a shiver

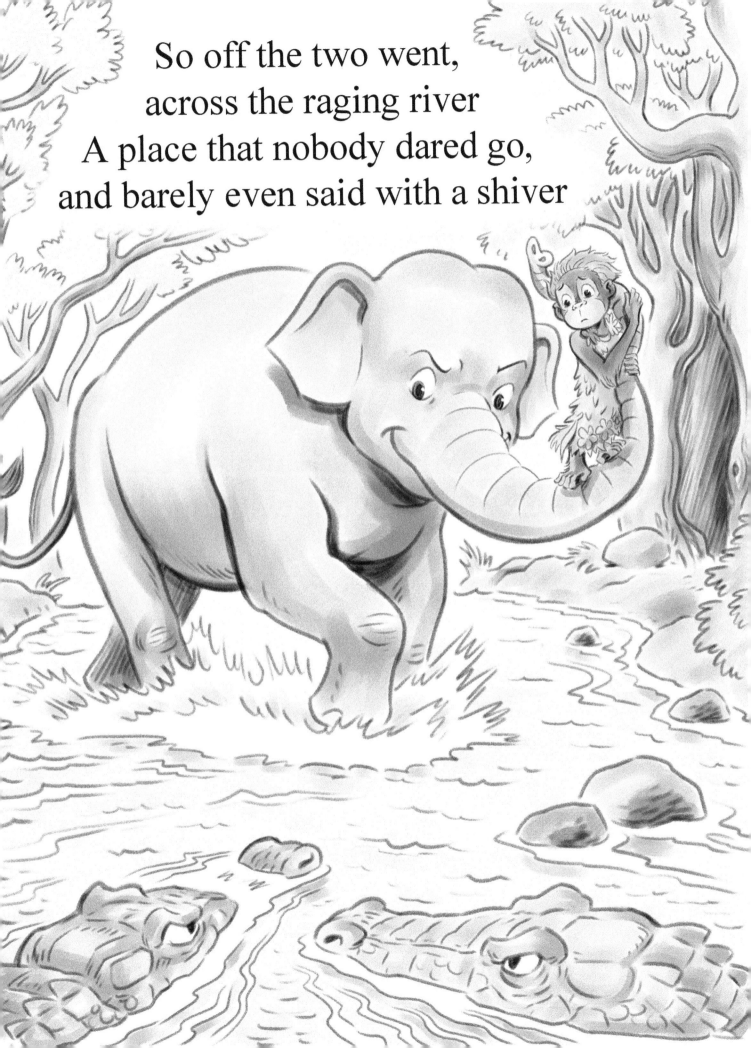

When they reached the cliff's edge,
Aviva had a plan

She would slide down Sofia's trunk
and swing with one hand

Up upon high they could see
lots of bananas below
Her heart pumping yet fearless,
she was ready to go!

Whoosh! Went Aviva.
She flew through the air,

Landing ever so gently
where others don't dare.

She perched on the treetop
and searched upon high

Until, at long last,
the golden fruit caught her eye.

Lurking below was what others feared most: An animal mean enough to scare a ghost!

Bright yellow eyes peered up from far beneath. A menacing snarl showed off sharp, pointy teeth.

Aviva looked down. She had seen things far worse. Scared she was not of this loud, frightful curse.

The tiger, she knew, could become her new friend. *Just be yourself*, she thought. *Do not pretend.*

Tito the Tiger wagged his tail,
as if to give a warning sign

But soon became shocked
when he saw Aviva smiling in the sunshine

Aviva began to sing, rhythmic and sweet. Far below, Tito's feet swayed to the beat.

What first was a shuffle
became a full-out dance.

"Wheeee!!" he said,
moving his feet in a prance

He grooved to the music;
he howled out with glee.

Now, Aviva was excited
to climb down that tree.

Aviva said,
"Move your body like this, Okie Dokie?"

Soon they were dancing a mix
between salsa and the Hokey Pokey.

Beep Boppity Doo-Wap Beep Bam Boom!
The orangutan and the tiger
were having a party at high noon!

They shook their hands, waved their tails,
then stomped their feet,
The new pals were working up a sweat
under tropical heat.

Soon they got hungry
and realized it was time to eat.

Taking a break,
Tito offered up a piece of meat.

"Can I have a banana?" Aviva said, "Please?"
"And maybe some extra to bring
'cross the trees?"

Aviva was proud,
she'd remembered her task.
"Of course," Tito said,
"all you had to do was ask."

They smiled at each other
as they both scarfed them down
Putting her arms around him, Aviva said
"You're the coolest tiger in town!"

So a friendship was born
over snacks and a song

Because Aviva was brave,
her family wouldn't be hungry for long

As she walked back with Sofia,
she was glad to go home

The best things in life
can't be accomplished alone

But above all,
Aviva the Diva
was true to herself

And at the end of the day,
that's what matters most,
above everything else.

About the Book

Aviva Lilia Bernardo Kullberg lived with
charm, grace, courage, fearlessness and joy during
her 10 months on earth. She exuded a radiant smile
filled with contagious laughter, dancing
to her brother's and sister's musical harmonies.
She had a zest for life, overcoming many obstacles
and loved her friends and family immensely.
Always a hungry eater, Aviva loved
all types of food, especially bananas.

This story is a love tribute by a
brokenhearted father to his dear baby girl.
It is his hope that it will bring smiles
of joy to children around the world.

Share your Smile on Facebook, Instagram & Twitter
with the hashtag #BabyAviva.

Learn more about the impact Aviva is creating at
hanskullberg.com

CPSIA information can be obtained
at www.ICGtesting.com
Printed in the USA
LVHW071026220122
709114LV00002B/15